# 50 Sweet and Savory Breakfast Recipes for Home

By: Kelly Johnson

# Table of Contents

- Blueberry Pancakes
- Spinach and Feta Omelette
- French Toast with Maple Syrup
- Breakfast Burrito with Eggs and Salsa
- Banana Bread
- Avocado Toast with Cherry Tomatoes
- Chocolate Chip Muffins
- Savory Oatmeal with Fried Egg
- Cinnamon Roll Casserole
- Smoked Salmon Bagel
- Fruit Smoothie Bowl
- Quiche Lorraine
- Overnight Chia Pudding with Berries
- Breakfast Quesadilla with Cheese
- Almond Joy Overnight Oats
- Zucchini Fritters with Yogurt Sauce
- Strawberry Waffles
- Sweet Potato Hash with Eggs
- Coconut Pancakes with Pineapple
- Egg and Bacon Breakfast Sandwich
- Nut Butter and Banana Toast
- Caramelized Apple Dutch Baby
- Greek Yogurt Parfait with Granola
- Savory Breakfast Polenta
- Berry Compote with Ricotta
- Egg and Cheese Breakfast Wrap
- Raspberry Almond Croissant Bake
- Huevos Rancheros
- Chocolate Banana Smoothie
- Quinoa Breakfast Bowl with Almonds
- Maple Pecan Granola
- Tomato and Basil Frittata
- Berry Crepes with Whipped Cream
- Spinach and Mushroom Breakfast Strata
- Lemon Poppy Seed Muffins

- Sausage and Egg Breakfast Casserole
- Oatmeal Cookies with Raisins
- Caprese Breakfast Sandwich
- Honey Yogurt with Fresh Fruit
- Pumpkin Spice Pancakes
- Savory Breakfast Scones
- Egg White and Veggie Scramble
- Nutella Stuffed French Toast
- Breakfast Tacos with Avocado
- Churros with Chocolate Sauce
- Broccoli and Cheddar Frittata
- Coconut Macadamia Granola Bars
- Carrot Cake Muffins
- Breakfast Fried Rice
- Berry Smoothie with Spinach

**Blueberry Pancakes**
**Ingredients:**

- 1 cup all-purpose flour
- 2 tablespoons sugar
- 1 tablespoon baking powder
- ½ teaspoon salt
- 1 cup milk
- 1 large egg
- 2 tablespoons melted butter
- 1 cup fresh blueberries

**Instructions:**

1. **Mix Dry Ingredients:** In a bowl, whisk together flour, sugar, baking powder, and salt.
2. **Combine Wet Ingredients:** In another bowl, mix milk, egg, and melted butter.
3. **Combine Mixtures:** Pour wet ingredients into dry ingredients and stir until just combined. Gently fold in blueberries.
4. **Cook Pancakes:** Heat a griddle or skillet over medium heat. Pour batter to form pancakes and cook until bubbles form, then flip and cook until golden.
5. **Serve:** Serve warm with syrup or toppings of choice.

**Spinach and Feta Omelette**
**Ingredients:**

- 2 large eggs
- 1 cup fresh spinach (chopped)
- ¼ cup feta cheese (crumbled)
- Salt and pepper to taste
- 1 tablespoon olive oil

**Instructions:**

1. **Whisk Eggs:** In a bowl, whisk together eggs, salt, and pepper.
2. **Sauté Spinach:** In a skillet, heat olive oil over medium heat. Add spinach and cook until wilted.
3. **Cook Omelette:** Pour eggs over spinach and cook until set. Sprinkle feta on one half and fold the omelette.
4. **Serve:** Slide onto a plate and enjoy your omelette!

**French Toast with Maple Syrup**
**Ingredients:**

- 2 slices bread (thick-cut)
- 1 large egg
- ¼ cup milk
- ½ teaspoon vanilla extract
- 1 teaspoon cinnamon (optional)
- Butter for cooking
- Maple syrup for serving

**Instructions:**

1. **Mix Batter:** In a bowl, whisk together egg, milk, vanilla, and cinnamon.
2. **Dip Bread:** Dip each slice of bread into the mixture, allowing it to soak for a moment.
3. **Cook French Toast:** In a skillet, melt butter over medium heat and cook each slice until golden on both sides.
4. **Serve:** Serve with maple syrup on top.

**Breakfast Burrito with Eggs and Salsa**
**Ingredients:**

- 2 large eggs
- 1 small tortilla
- ¼ cup salsa
- ¼ avocado (sliced)
- Salt and pepper to taste
- 1 tablespoon olive oil

**Instructions:**

1. **Scramble Eggs:** In a bowl, whisk eggs with salt and pepper.
2. **Cook Eggs:** In a skillet, heat olive oil over medium heat and scramble the eggs until cooked through.
3. **Assemble Burrito:** Place scrambled eggs on the tortilla, top with salsa and avocado, and roll it up.
4. **Serve:** Enjoy your delicious breakfast burrito!

**Banana Bread**
**Ingredients:**

- 3 ripe bananas (mashed)
- ½ cup sugar
- 1/3 cup melted butter
- 1 large egg
- 1 teaspoon vanilla extract
- 1 teaspoon baking soda
- Pinch of salt
- 1 cup all-purpose flour

**Instructions:**

1. **Preheat Oven:** Preheat the oven to 350°F (175°C) and grease a loaf pan.
2. **Mix Ingredients:** In a bowl, mix mashed bananas with melted butter. Stir in sugar, egg, and vanilla. Add baking soda and salt, then mix in flour.
3. **Bake:** Pour batter into the prepared loaf pan and bake for 50-60 minutes, until a toothpick comes out clean.
4. **Cool and Serve:** Allow to cool before slicing and enjoying!

**Avocado Toast with Cherry Tomatoes**
**Ingredients:**

- 1 slice whole grain bread
- ½ avocado (mashed)
- ¼ cup cherry tomatoes (halved)
- Salt and pepper to taste
- Olive oil (optional)

**Instructions:**

1. **Toast Bread:** Toast the slice of bread until golden.
2. **Spread Avocado:** Spread mashed avocado on the toasted bread and season with salt and pepper.
3. **Top with Tomatoes:** Top with halved cherry tomatoes and drizzle with olive oil if desired.
4. **Serve:** Enjoy your fresh avocado toast!

**Chocolate Chip Muffins**
**Ingredients:**

- 1 ½ cups all-purpose flour
- ½ cup sugar
- 1 tablespoon baking powder
- ½ teaspoon salt
- 1 cup milk
- 1/3 cup vegetable oil
- 1 large egg
- 1 cup chocolate chips

**Instructions:**

1. **Preheat Oven:** Preheat the oven to 375°F (190°C) and line a muffin tin with paper liners.
2. **Mix Dry Ingredients:** In a bowl, whisk together flour, sugar, baking powder, and salt.
3. **Combine Wet Ingredients:** In another bowl, mix milk, oil, and egg.
4. **Combine Mixtures:** Pour wet ingredients into dry ingredients and stir until just combined. Fold in chocolate chips.
5. **Bake Muffins:** Fill muffin cups and bake for 18-20 minutes, or until a toothpick comes out clean.
6. **Cool and Serve:** Allow to cool before enjoying your delicious muffins!

**Savory Oatmeal with Fried Egg**
**Ingredients:**

- 1 cup rolled oats
- 2 cups vegetable broth or water
- 1 large egg
- ½ avocado (sliced)
- Salt and pepper to taste
- Optional toppings: green onions, hot sauce, cheese

**Instructions:**

1. **Cook Oats:** In a saucepan, bring vegetable broth or water to a boil. Add oats and cook according to package instructions until creamy.
2. **Fry Egg:** In a skillet, fry the egg to your desired doneness.
3. **Assemble Bowl:** Serve the savory oatmeal in a bowl, top with the fried egg, avocado slices, and any additional toppings.
4. **Season and Serve:** Season with salt and pepper and enjoy your savory breakfast!

**Cinnamon Roll Casserole**
**Ingredients:**

- 2 cans refrigerated cinnamon rolls
- 4 large eggs
- ½ cup milk
- 1 teaspoon vanilla extract
- 1 teaspoon cinnamon
- Optional: frosting from cinnamon rolls

**Instructions:**

1. **Preheat Oven:** Preheat the oven to 350°F (175°C) and grease a baking dish.
2. **Prepare Cinnamon Rolls:** Cut the cinnamon rolls into quarters and place them in the baking dish.
3. **Mix Eggs:** In a bowl, whisk together eggs, milk, vanilla, and cinnamon. Pour over the cinnamon roll pieces.
4. **Bake:** Bake for 25-30 minutes, until golden and cooked through.
5. **Add Frosting:** Drizzle frosting over the top and serve warm.

**Smoked Salmon Bagel**
**Ingredients:**

- 1 bagel (any flavor)
- 2 ounces smoked salmon
- 2 tablespoons cream cheese
- ¼ avocado (sliced)
- Capers and red onion (optional)
- Fresh dill (for garnish)

**Instructions:**

1. **Toast Bagel:** Toast the bagel until golden.
2. **Spread Cream Cheese:** Spread cream cheese evenly on both halves of the bagel.
3. **Layer Ingredients:** Top with smoked salmon, avocado slices, capers, and red onion if desired.
4. **Serve:** Garnish with fresh dill and enjoy your bagel!

**Fruit Smoothie Bowl**
**Ingredients:**

- 1 banana (frozen)
- 1 cup mixed berries (frozen or fresh)
- ½ cup yogurt (Greek or regular)
- ½ cup milk or almond milk
- Toppings: sliced fruit, granola, nuts, seeds

**Instructions:**

1. **Blend Smoothie:** In a blender, combine banana, berries, yogurt, and milk. Blend until smooth and creamy.
2. **Assemble Bowl:** Pour the smoothie into a bowl.
3. **Add Toppings:** Top with sliced fruit, granola, nuts, or seeds as desired.
4. **Serve:** Enjoy your refreshing smoothie bowl!

**Quiche Lorraine**
**Ingredients:**

- 1 pie crust (store-bought or homemade)
- 6 large eggs
- 1 cup heavy cream
- 1 cup shredded Swiss cheese
- ½ cup cooked bacon (crumbled)
- Salt and pepper to taste

**Instructions:**

1. **Preheat Oven:** Preheat the oven to 375°F (190°C).
2. **Prepare Filling:** In a bowl, whisk together eggs, heavy cream, salt, and pepper. Stir in cheese and bacon.
3. **Assemble Quiche:** Pour the filling into the pie crust.
4. **Bake:** Bake for 35-40 minutes, until the quiche is set and golden.
5. **Cool and Serve:** Allow to cool slightly before slicing and serving.

**Overnight Chia Pudding with Berries**

**Ingredients:**

- ¼ cup chia seeds
- 1 cup milk (dairy or plant-based)
- 1 tablespoon honey or maple syrup
- 1 cup mixed berries

**Instructions:**

1. **Mix Ingredients:** In a bowl, combine chia seeds, milk, and honey. Stir well.
2. **Refrigerate:** Cover and refrigerate overnight or for at least 4 hours until it thickens.
3. **Serve:** Top with mixed berries before serving. Enjoy your nutritious chia pudding!

**Breakfast Quesadilla with Cheese**
**Ingredients:**

- 2 large tortillas
- 1 cup shredded cheese (cheddar, mozzarella, or your choice)
- 2 large eggs
- 1 tablespoon olive oil
- Optional fillings: cooked vegetables, ham, or salsa

**Instructions:**

1. **Cook Eggs:** In a skillet, heat olive oil and scramble the eggs until cooked.
2. **Assemble Quesadilla:** On one tortilla, layer cheese, scrambled eggs, and any optional fillings. Top with the second tortilla.
3. **Cook Quesadilla:** In the skillet, cook the quesadilla until golden and crispy, flipping once.
4. **Serve:** Cut into wedges and serve with salsa or sour cream if desired.

**Almond Joy Overnight Oats**
**Ingredients:**

- ½ cup rolled oats
- 1 cup almond milk
- 1 tablespoon cocoa powder
- 1 tablespoon shredded coconut
- 1 tablespoon honey or maple syrup
- 2 tablespoons chopped almonds

**Instructions:**

1. **Combine Ingredients:** In a jar or bowl, mix oats, almond milk, cocoa powder, coconut, and sweetener.
2. **Refrigerate:** Cover and refrigerate overnight.
3. **Add Toppings:** In the morning, stir and top with chopped almonds. Enjoy your delicious overnight oats!

**Zucchini Fritters with Yogurt Sauce**
**Ingredients:**

- 2 medium zucchini (grated)
- 1 teaspoon salt
- ½ cup all-purpose flour
- 2 large eggs
- ¼ cup grated Parmesan cheese
- 2 green onions (chopped)
- ½ teaspoon garlic powder
- Olive oil for frying
- **For the Yogurt Sauce:**
- 1 cup Greek yogurt
- 1 tablespoon lemon juice
- Salt and pepper to taste

**Instructions:**

1. **Prepare Zucchini:** In a bowl, sprinkle grated zucchini with salt and let sit for 10 minutes. Squeeze out excess moisture.
2. **Mix Fritter Ingredients:** In a mixing bowl, combine zucchini, flour, eggs, Parmesan, green onions, and garlic powder.
3. **Fry Fritters:** Heat olive oil in a skillet over medium heat. Drop spoonfuls of the mixture into the skillet and flatten slightly. Cook until golden on both sides.
4. **Prepare Yogurt Sauce:** In a small bowl, mix Greek yogurt, lemon juice, salt, and pepper.
5. **Serve:** Serve fritters warm with yogurt sauce on the side.

**Strawberry Waffles**
**Ingredients:**

- 1 ½ cups all-purpose flour
- 2 tablespoons sugar
- 1 tablespoon baking powder
- ½ teaspoon salt
- 1 ¾ cups milk
- ½ cup vegetable oil
- 2 large eggs
- 1 cup fresh strawberries (sliced)

**Instructions:**

1. **Preheat Waffle Iron:** Preheat your waffle iron according to manufacturer instructions.
2. **Mix Dry Ingredients:** In a large bowl, whisk together flour, sugar, baking powder, and salt.
3. **Combine Wet Ingredients:** In another bowl, mix milk, vegetable oil, and eggs.
4. **Combine Mixtures:** Pour the wet ingredients into the dry ingredients and stir until just combined. Fold in sliced strawberries.
5. **Cook Waffles:** Pour batter into the preheated waffle iron and cook until golden and crisp.
6. **Serve:** Serve with additional strawberries and syrup if desired.

**Sweet Potato Hash with Eggs**
**Ingredients:**

- 2 medium sweet potatoes (peeled and diced)
- 1 red bell pepper (diced)
- 1 onion (diced)
- 2 tablespoons olive oil
- 4 large eggs
- Salt and pepper to taste
- Optional: fresh herbs for garnish

**Instructions:**

1. **Cook Vegetables:** In a large skillet, heat olive oil over medium heat. Add sweet potatoes, bell pepper, and onion. Cook until sweet potatoes are tender and golden, about 10-15 minutes.
2. **Season:** Season with salt and pepper.
3. **Cook Eggs:** Make four wells in the hash and crack an egg into each well. Cover and cook until the eggs are set to your liking.
4. **Serve:** Garnish with fresh herbs if desired and serve warm.

**Coconut Pancakes with Pineapple**

**Ingredients:**

- 1 cup all-purpose flour
- 1 tablespoon baking powder
- ½ teaspoon salt
- 1 cup coconut milk
- 2 large eggs
- ¼ cup shredded coconut
- 1 cup fresh pineapple (diced)

**Instructions:**

1. **Mix Dry Ingredients:** In a bowl, whisk together flour, baking powder, and salt.
2. **Combine Wet Ingredients:** In another bowl, mix coconut milk and eggs.
3. **Combine Mixtures:** Pour wet ingredients into dry ingredients and stir until just combined. Fold in shredded coconut and diced pineapple.
4. **Cook Pancakes:** Heat a skillet over medium heat and pour batter to form pancakes. Cook until bubbles form, then flip and cook until golden.
5. **Serve:** Serve warm with extra pineapple and syrup if desired.

**Egg and Bacon Breakfast Sandwich**
**Ingredients:**

- 2 slices of bread or an English muffin
- 2 large eggs
- 2 slices of bacon
- 1 slice of cheese (optional)
- Butter for toasting
- Salt and pepper to taste

**Instructions:**

1. **Cook Bacon:** In a skillet, cook bacon until crispy. Remove and set aside.
2. **Cook Eggs:** In the same skillet, crack eggs and cook to your liking (sunny-side up, scrambled, etc.). Season with salt and pepper.
3. **Assemble Sandwich:** Toast the bread or English muffin in the skillet. Layer with bacon, egg, and cheese if using.
4. **Serve:** Serve warm and enjoy!

**Nut Butter and Banana Toast**
**Ingredients:**

- 1 slice whole grain bread
- 2 tablespoons nut butter (peanut, almond, etc.)
- ½ banana (sliced)
- Honey or maple syrup (optional)
- Chia seeds (for topping, optional)

**Instructions:**

1. **Toast Bread:** Toast the slice of bread until golden.
2. **Spread Nut Butter:** Spread nut butter evenly over the toasted bread.
3. **Top with Banana:** Arrange banana slices on top and drizzle with honey or maple syrup if desired.
4. **Serve:** Sprinkle chia seeds on top if using and enjoy your toast!

**Caramelized Apple Dutch Baby**

**Ingredients:**

- 3 apples (sliced)
- 2 tablespoons butter
- 2 tablespoons brown sugar
- 1 cup all-purpose flour
- 1 cup milk
- 3 large eggs
- 1 teaspoon vanilla extract
- ½ teaspoon cinnamon
- Powdered sugar for serving

**Instructions:**

1. **Preheat Oven:** Preheat the oven to 425°F (220°C).
2. **Caramelize Apples:** In a skillet, melt butter over medium heat. Add sliced apples and brown sugar, cooking until apples are tender and caramelized.
3. **Prepare Batter:** In a bowl, whisk together flour, milk, eggs, vanilla, and cinnamon until smooth.
4. **Bake Dutch Baby:** Pour the batter over the caramelized apples in the skillet and transfer to the oven. Bake for 20-25 minutes until puffed and golden.
5. **Serve:** Dust with powdered sugar before serving warm.

**Greek Yogurt Parfait with Granola**

**Ingredients:**

- 2 cups Greek yogurt
- 1 cup granola
- 1 cup mixed berries (strawberries, blueberries, raspberries)
- Honey or maple syrup (optional)

**Instructions:**

1. **Layer Ingredients:** In a glass or bowl, layer Greek yogurt, granola, and mixed berries.
2. **Repeat Layers:** Repeat the layers until all ingredients are used, finishing with a layer of berries on top.
3. **Drizzle:** Drizzle with honey or maple syrup if desired.
4. **Serve:** Serve immediately for a fresh breakfast.

**Savory Breakfast Polenta**

**Ingredients:**

- 1 cup cornmeal
- 4 cups water or vegetable broth
- ½ teaspoon salt
- 1 cup cooked spinach
- 2 eggs (poached or fried)
- Grated Parmesan cheese (for topping)
- Black pepper to taste

**Instructions:**

1. **Cook Polenta:** In a pot, bring water or broth to a boil. Gradually whisk in cornmeal and salt, stirring constantly until thickened (about 5 minutes).
2. **Add Spinach:** Stir in cooked spinach and cook for another minute.
3. **Serve:** Spoon polenta into bowls, top with a poached or fried egg, grated Parmesan, and black pepper.

**Berry Compote with Ricotta**
**Ingredients:**

- 2 cups mixed berries (fresh or frozen)
- 2 tablespoons sugar
- 1 tablespoon lemon juice
- 1 cup ricotta cheese
- Mint leaves (for garnish)

**Instructions:**

1. **Make Compote:** In a saucepan, combine berries, sugar, and lemon juice. Cook over medium heat until berries break down and sauce thickens (about 5-10 minutes).
2. **Serve:** In a bowl, spoon ricotta cheese and top with warm berry compote.
3. **Garnish:** Garnish with mint leaves and serve.

**Egg and Cheese Breakfast Wrap**
**Ingredients:**

- 2 large eggs
- 1 tablespoon milk
- Salt and pepper to taste
- 1 whole wheat tortilla
- ¼ cup shredded cheese (cheddar or your choice)
- Salsa (for serving)

**Instructions:**

1. **Scramble Eggs:** In a bowl, whisk together eggs, milk, salt, and pepper. Pour into a skillet over medium heat, cooking until scrambled.
2. **Assemble Wrap:** Place scrambled eggs in the center of the tortilla, sprinkle with cheese, and fold the sides over to wrap.
3. **Heat Wrap:** Return to the skillet and cook for 1-2 minutes on each side until heated through and cheese melts.
4. **Serve:** Serve warm with salsa on the side.

**Raspberry Almond Croissant Bake**
**Ingredients:**

- 4 croissants (day-old or stale)
- 2 cups raspberries
- 4 large eggs
- 1 cup milk
- ½ cup almond milk
- ½ cup sugar
- 1 teaspoon vanilla extract
- Sliced almonds (for topping)

**Instructions:**

1. **Preheat Oven:** Preheat the oven to 350°F (175°C).
2. **Prepare Croissants:** Tear croissants into pieces and place in a greased baking dish. Scatter raspberries on top.
3. **Make Custard:** In a bowl, whisk together eggs, milk, almond milk, sugar, and vanilla. Pour over croissants and raspberries.
4. **Bake:** Top with sliced almonds and bake for 30-35 minutes until set and golden.
5. **Serve:** Serve warm, optionally with whipped cream.

**Huevos Rancheros**

**Ingredients:**

- 4 corn tortillas
- 4 large eggs
- 1 cup black beans (canned or cooked)
- 1 cup salsa
- ¼ cup crumbled queso fresco or feta cheese
- Fresh cilantro (for garnish)

**Instructions:**

1. **Heat Tortillas:** In a skillet, warm tortillas over medium heat until pliable.
2. **Cook Eggs:** In the same skillet, crack eggs and cook to your liking (sunny-side up or over-easy).
3. **Assemble Dish:** On each tortilla, layer black beans, an egg, and salsa.
4. **Garnish:** Sprinkle with queso fresco and cilantro. Serve warm.

**Chocolate Banana Smoothie**
**Ingredients:**

- 2 ripe bananas
- 1 cup milk (dairy or non-dairy)
- 2 tablespoons cocoa powder
- 1 tablespoon honey or maple syrup
- ½ teaspoon vanilla extract
- Ice cubes (optional)

**Instructions:**

1. **Blend Ingredients:** In a blender, combine bananas, milk, cocoa powder, honey, and vanilla. Blend until smooth.
2. **Add Ice:** If desired, add ice cubes and blend again for a chilled smoothie.
3. **Serve:** Pour into glasses and serve immediately.

**Quinoa Breakfast Bowl with Almonds**

**Ingredients:**

- 1 cup cooked quinoa
- 1 cup almond milk (or any milk of choice)
- ¼ cup almonds (sliced or chopped)
- 1 tablespoon honey or maple syrup
- ½ teaspoon cinnamon
- Fresh fruit (berries, banana, etc., for topping)

**Instructions:**

1. **Heat Quinoa:** In a saucepan, combine cooked quinoa and almond milk. Heat over medium heat until warmed through.
2. **Mix in Sweetener:** Stir in honey (or maple syrup) and cinnamon.
3. **Serve:** Transfer to a bowl, top with almonds and fresh fruit.

**Maple Pecan Granola**
**Ingredients:**

- 3 cups rolled oats
- 1 cup pecans (chopped)
- ½ cup maple syrup
- ½ cup coconut oil (melted)
- 1 teaspoon vanilla extract
- ½ teaspoon salt
- ½ teaspoon cinnamon

**Instructions:**

1. **Preheat Oven:** Preheat the oven to 350°F (175°C).
2. **Mix Ingredients:** In a large bowl, combine oats, pecans, maple syrup, melted coconut oil, vanilla, salt, and cinnamon. Mix well.
3. **Bake Granola:** Spread mixture onto a baking sheet and bake for 25-30 minutes, stirring halfway through until golden brown.
4. **Cool and Store:** Let cool completely and store in an airtight container.

**Tomato and Basil Frittata**
**Ingredients:**

- 6 large eggs
- ½ cup milk
- 1 cup cherry tomatoes (halved)
- ¼ cup fresh basil (chopped)
- ½ cup feta cheese (crumbled)
- Salt and pepper to taste
- Olive oil for cooking

**Instructions:**

1. **Preheat Oven:** Preheat the oven to 350°F (175°C).
2. **Whisk Eggs:** In a bowl, whisk together eggs, milk, salt, and pepper.
3. **Combine Ingredients:** Stir in cherry tomatoes, basil, and feta.
4. **Cook Frittata:** Heat olive oil in an oven-safe skillet over medium heat. Pour in the egg mixture and cook for 5 minutes until edges start to set.
5. **Finish in Oven:** Transfer skillet to the oven and bake for 15-20 minutes until the frittata is set.
6. **Serve:** Slice and serve warm or at room temperature.

**Berry Crepes with Whipped Cream**
**Ingredients:**

- **For the Crepes:**
    - 1 cup all-purpose flour
    - 2 large eggs
    - 1 ½ cups milk
    - 2 tablespoons melted butter
    - 1 tablespoon sugar
    - ½ teaspoon vanilla extract
- **For the Filling:**
    - 1 cup mixed berries (strawberries, blueberries, raspberries)
    - Whipped cream for serving

**Instructions:**

1. **Make Crepe Batter:** In a bowl, whisk together flour, eggs, milk, melted butter, sugar, and vanilla until smooth. Let sit for 30 minutes.
2. **Cook Crepes:** Heat a non-stick skillet over medium heat. Pour in a ladle of batter, swirling to coat the bottom. Cook for 1-2 minutes until edges lift, then flip and cook for another minute. Repeat with remaining batter.
3. **Fill Crepes:** Fill each crepe with mixed berries and fold or roll.
4. **Serve:** Top with whipped cream before serving.

**Spinach and Mushroom Breakfast Strata**
**Ingredients:**

- 6 slices whole grain bread (cubed)
- 2 cups fresh spinach (chopped)
- 1 cup mushrooms (sliced)
- 6 large eggs
- 2 cups milk
- 1 cup shredded cheese (cheddar or your choice)
- Salt and pepper to taste

**Instructions:**

1. **Preheat Oven:** Preheat the oven to 350°F (175°C).
2. **Sauté Vegetables:** In a skillet, sauté mushrooms and spinach until soft.
3. **Combine Ingredients:** In a bowl, whisk together eggs, milk, salt, and pepper. Add bread cubes, sautéed vegetables, and cheese. Mix well.
4. **Bake Strata:** Pour mixture into a greased baking dish and bake for 30-35 minutes until set and golden.
5. **Serve:** Let cool slightly before slicing and serving.

**Lemon Poppy Seed Muffins**
**Ingredients:**

- 1 ½ cups all-purpose flour
- 1 teaspoon baking powder
- ½ teaspoon baking soda
- ½ teaspoon salt
- ½ cup sugar
- ½ cup vegetable oil
- 2 large eggs
- ½ cup buttermilk
- Zest of 1 lemon
- 2 tablespoons lemon juice
- 2 tablespoons poppy seeds

**Instructions:**

1. **Preheat Oven:** Preheat the oven to 350°F (175°C). Line a muffin tin with paper liners.
2. **Mix Dry Ingredients:** In a bowl, whisk together flour, baking powder, baking soda, salt, and sugar.
3. **Combine Wet Ingredients:** In another bowl, mix oil, eggs, buttermilk, lemon zest, and lemon juice.
4. **Combine Mixtures:** Add wet ingredients to dry ingredients and stir until just combined. Fold in poppy seeds.
5. **Bake Muffins:** Divide batter among muffin cups and bake for 18-20 minutes until a toothpick comes out clean.
6. **Cool and Serve:** Let cool in the pan for a few minutes before transferring to a wire rack.

**Sausage and Egg Breakfast Casserole**
**Ingredients:**

- 1 pound breakfast sausage (casings removed)
- 6 large eggs
- 2 cups milk
- 1 cup shredded cheese (cheddar or your choice)
- 1 teaspoon salt
- ½ teaspoon pepper
- 4 cups cubed bread (day-old works best)
- Optional: chopped bell peppers or onions

**Instructions:**

1. **Preheat Oven:** Preheat the oven to 350°F (175°C).
2. **Cook Sausage:** In a skillet, cook sausage until browned. Drain excess fat.
3. **Combine Ingredients:** In a bowl, whisk together eggs, milk, salt, and pepper. Add bread cubes, sausage, and cheese (and any vegetables if using).
4. **Bake Casserole:** Pour mixture into a greased baking dish and bake for 30-40 minutes until set.
5. **Serve:** Let cool for a few minutes before slicing and serving.

**Oatmeal Cookies with Raisins**

**Ingredients:**

- 1 cup butter (softened)
- 1 cup brown sugar
- ½ cup granulated sugar
- 2 large eggs
- 1 teaspoon vanilla extract
- 1 ½ cups all-purpose flour
- 1 teaspoon baking soda
- ½ teaspoon salt
- 3 cups rolled oats
- 1 cup raisins

**Instructions:**

1. **Preheat Oven:** Preheat the oven to 350°F (175°C).
2. **Cream Butter and Sugars:** In a bowl, cream together softened butter, brown sugar, and granulated sugar until light and fluffy.
3. **Add Eggs and Vanilla:** Beat in eggs one at a time, then stir in vanilla.
4. **Combine Dry Ingredients:** In another bowl, whisk together flour, baking soda, and salt. Gradually add to the butter mixture, mixing well.
5. **Stir in Oats and Raisins:** Fold in rolled oats and raisins.
6. **Bake Cookies:** Drop spoonfuls of dough onto baking sheets and bake for 10-12 minutes until golden.
7. **Cool and Serve:** Let cool on the baking sheets for a few minutes before transferring to wire racks.

**Caprese Breakfast Sandwich**
**Ingredients:**

- 1 whole grain English muffin (split and toasted)
- 1 large egg (fried or poached)
- 1 slice fresh mozzarella cheese
- 2-3 slices of ripe tomato
- Fresh basil leaves
- Balsamic glaze (optional)
- Salt and pepper to taste

**Instructions:**

1. **Cook Egg:** Cook the egg to your liking (fried or poached).
2. **Assemble Sandwich:** On the bottom half of the toasted English muffin, layer the mozzarella slice, tomato slices, and basil leaves. Top with the cooked egg.
3. **Season:** Drizzle with balsamic glaze, if desired, and season with salt and pepper.
4. **Serve:** Place the top half of the muffin on and serve immediately.

**Honey Yogurt with Fresh Fruit**
**Ingredients:**

- 1 cup plain Greek yogurt
- 2 tablespoons honey
- 1 cup mixed fresh fruit (berries, banana, kiwi, etc.)
- 2 tablespoons granola (optional)

**Instructions:**

1. **Prepare Yogurt:** In a bowl, combine the Greek yogurt and honey. Mix until well combined.
2. **Add Fruit:** Top the yogurt with mixed fresh fruit.
3. **Garnish:** Sprinkle with granola if desired.
4. **Serve:** Enjoy immediately as a refreshing breakfast or snack.

**Pumpkin Spice Pancakes**
**Ingredients:**

- 1 cup all-purpose flour
- 2 tablespoons sugar
- 1 teaspoon baking powder
- ½ teaspoon baking soda
- ½ teaspoon salt
- 1 teaspoon pumpkin pie spice
- 1 cup buttermilk
- 1 cup pumpkin puree
- 1 large egg
- 2 tablespoons melted butter

**Instructions:**

1. **Mix Dry Ingredients:** In a bowl, whisk together flour, sugar, baking powder, baking soda, salt, and pumpkin pie spice.
2. **Combine Wet Ingredients:** In another bowl, mix buttermilk, pumpkin puree, egg, and melted butter.
3. **Combine Mixtures:** Pour the wet ingredients into the dry ingredients and stir until just combined.
4. **Cook Pancakes:** Heat a non-stick skillet over medium heat. Pour batter onto the skillet and cook until bubbles form on the surface, then flip and cook until golden brown.
5. **Serve:** Serve warm with maple syrup.

**Savory Breakfast Scones**
**Ingredients:**

- 2 cups all-purpose flour
- 1 tablespoon baking powder
- ½ teaspoon salt
- ½ cup cold butter (cubed)
- 1 cup shredded cheese (cheddar or your choice)
- ½ cup cooked bacon or sausage (crumbled)
- ¼ cup green onions (chopped)
- ¾ cup milk

**Instructions:**

1. **Preheat Oven:** Preheat the oven to 400°F (200°C).
2. **Mix Dry Ingredients:** In a bowl, combine flour, baking powder, and salt.
3. **Cut in Butter:** Add cubed cold butter and mix until the mixture resembles coarse crumbs.
4. **Add Cheese and Meats:** Stir in cheese, crumbled bacon or sausage, and green onions.
5. **Combine Mixture:** Gradually add milk until a dough forms.
6. **Shape and Bake:** Turn dough onto a floured surface and pat into a circle about 1 inch thick. Cut into wedges and place on a baking sheet. Bake for 15-20 minutes until golden brown.

**Egg White and Veggie Scramble**
**Ingredients:**

- 4 egg whites
- 1 cup mixed vegetables (spinach, bell peppers, onions, etc.)
- ¼ cup feta cheese (crumbled)
- Salt and pepper to taste
- Olive oil for cooking

**Instructions:**

1. **Sauté Vegetables:** In a skillet, heat olive oil over medium heat. Add mixed vegetables and sauté until tender.
2. **Add Egg Whites:** Pour in egg whites and cook, stirring gently until scrambled and cooked through.
3. **Add Cheese:** Stir in feta cheese and season with salt and pepper.
4. **Serve:** Serve warm, either alone or on a whole grain toast.

**Nutella Stuffed French Toast**
**Ingredients:**

- 4 slices of bread (thick-cut, like brioche)
- ¼ cup Nutella
- 2 large eggs
- ½ cup milk
- 1 teaspoon vanilla extract
- 1 tablespoon cinnamon (optional)
- Butter for cooking

**Instructions:**

1. **Prepare Sandwiches:** Spread Nutella between two slices of bread to make a sandwich.
2. **Mix Egg Mixture:** In a bowl, whisk together eggs, milk, vanilla extract, and cinnamon (if using).
3. **Dip Sandwiches:** Dip each sandwich into the egg mixture, coating both sides.
4. **Cook French Toast:** In a skillet, melt butter over medium heat. Cook sandwiches for 3-4 minutes on each side until golden brown.
5. **Serve:** Serve warm with powdered sugar or syrup.

**Breakfast Tacos with Avocado**
**Ingredients:**

- 4 small corn or flour tortillas
- 4 large eggs
- 1 avocado (sliced)
- ½ cup salsa
- Fresh cilantro (for garnish)
- Salt and pepper to taste

**Instructions:**

1. **Cook Eggs:** Scramble or fry eggs in a skillet and season with salt and pepper.
2. **Warm Tortillas:** Warm tortillas in another skillet or microwave.
3. **Assemble Tacos:** Fill each tortilla with scrambled eggs, avocado slices, and salsa.
4. **Garnish:** Sprinkle with fresh cilantro and serve immediately.

**Churros with Chocolate Sauce**
**Ingredients:**

- 1 cup water
- 1/2 cup unsalted butter
- 1 tablespoon sugar
- 1/4 teaspoon salt
- 1 cup all-purpose flour
- 2 large eggs
- 1 teaspoon vanilla extract
- Oil for frying
- 1/2 cup sugar (for coating)
- 1 teaspoon cinnamon

**For Chocolate Sauce:**

- 1 cup dark chocolate chips
- 1/2 cup heavy cream

**Instructions:**

1. **Make Dough:** In a saucepan, combine water, butter, sugar, and salt. Bring to a boil. Remove from heat and stir in flour until a dough forms. Let cool slightly, then add eggs and vanilla, mixing until smooth.
2. **Heat Oil:** Heat oil in a deep skillet to 375°F (190°C).
3. **Pipe Churros:** Transfer dough to a piping bag fitted with a star tip. Pipe 6-inch lengths into the hot oil, cutting with scissors. Fry until golden brown, about 2-3 minutes per side.
4. **Coat Churros:** Remove and drain on paper towels, then roll in a mixture of sugar and cinnamon.
5. **Make Chocolate Sauce:** In a small saucepan, heat heavy cream until simmering. Pour over chocolate chips and let sit for 2 minutes. Stir until smooth.
6. **Serve:** Serve churros warm with chocolate sauce for dipping.

## Broccoli and Cheddar Frittata
**Ingredients:**

- 6 large eggs
- 1 cup broccoli florets (steamed)
- 1 cup shredded cheddar cheese
- 1/4 cup milk
- Salt and pepper to taste
- 1 tablespoon olive oil

**Instructions:**

1. **Preheat Oven:** Preheat the oven to 375°F (190°C).
2. **Whisk Eggs:** In a bowl, whisk together eggs, milk, salt, and pepper.
3. **Cook Broccoli:** In an oven-safe skillet, heat olive oil over medium heat. Add steamed broccoli and sauté for 1-2 minutes.
4. **Add Eggs and Cheese:** Pour the egg mixture over the broccoli and sprinkle with cheese.
5. **Bake:** Cook on the stovetop for 2-3 minutes until the edges begin to set, then transfer to the oven and bake for 15-20 minutes until set.
6. **Serve:** Let cool slightly, slice, and serve warm.

## Coconut Macadamia Granola Bars
**Ingredients:**

- 2 cups rolled oats
- 1 cup chopped macadamia nuts

- 1/2 cup shredded coconut
- 1/2 cup honey or maple syrup
- 1/4 cup coconut oil (melted)
- 1/2 teaspoon vanilla extract
- 1/4 teaspoon salt

**Instructions:**

1. **Preheat Oven:** Preheat the oven to 350°F (175°C). Line an 8x8-inch baking dish with parchment paper.
2. **Mix Ingredients:** In a large bowl, combine oats, macadamia nuts, coconut, honey, melted coconut oil, vanilla, and salt. Mix well.
3. **Press into Dish:** Press the mixture firmly into the prepared baking dish.
4. **Bake:** Bake for 20-25 minutes until golden. Let cool completely before cutting into bars.
5. **Serve:** Store in an airtight container for up to a week.

**Carrot Cake Muffins**

**Ingredients:**

- 1 cup whole wheat flour
- 1 teaspoon baking powder
- 1/2 teaspoon baking soda
- 1 teaspoon cinnamon
- 1/4 teaspoon salt
- 1/2 cup sugar
- 1/2 cup vegetable oil
- 2 large eggs
- 1 teaspoon vanilla extract
- 1 1/2 cups grated carrots
- 1/2 cup chopped walnuts (optional)

**Instructions:**

1. **Preheat Oven:** Preheat the oven to 350°F (175°C) and line a muffin tin with paper liners.
2. **Mix Dry Ingredients:** In a bowl, whisk together flour, baking powder, baking soda, cinnamon, and salt.
3. **Mix Wet Ingredients:** In another bowl, beat together sugar, oil, eggs, and vanilla until smooth.

4. **Combine Mixtures:** Stir the wet mixture into the dry ingredients until just combined. Fold in grated carrots and walnuts.
5. **Bake:** Divide the batter into the muffin cups and bake for 20-25 minutes or until a toothpick comes out clean.
6. **Serve:** Let cool before serving.

## Breakfast Fried Rice
**Ingredients:**

- 2 cups cooked rice (preferably day-old)
- 2 large eggs (beaten)
- 1 cup mixed vegetables (peas, carrots, bell peppers)
- 2 green onions (sliced)
- 2 tablespoons soy sauce
- 1 tablespoon sesame oil
- Salt and pepper to taste

**Instructions:**

1. **Cook Eggs:** In a large skillet or wok, heat sesame oil over medium heat. Add beaten eggs and scramble until fully cooked. Remove and set aside.
2. **Stir-fry Vegetables:** In the same skillet, add mixed vegetables and stir-fry for 2-3 minutes until tender.
3. **Add Rice:** Add the cooked rice, soy sauce, and green onions. Stir to combine and heat through.
4. **Combine Ingredients:** Add the scrambled eggs back to the skillet and mix well. Season with salt and pepper to taste.
5. **Serve:** Serve warm as a hearty breakfast.

## Berry Smoothie with Spinach
**Ingredients:**

- 1 cup frozen mixed berries
- 1 banana
- 1 cup spinach (fresh)
- 1/2 cup yogurt (plain or flavored)
- 1 cup almond milk (or milk of choice)
- 1 tablespoon honey (optional)

**Instructions:**

1. **Blend Ingredients:** In a blender, combine frozen berries, banana, spinach, yogurt, almond milk, and honey.
2. **Blend Until Smooth:** Blend until smooth and creamy, adding more milk if needed for desired consistency.
3. **Serve:** Pour into a glass and enjoy immediately.

www.ingramcontent.com/pod-product-compliance
Lightning Source LLC
LaVergne TN
LVHW081509060526
838201LV00056BA/3013